FESTIVE COOKIES

Drawn by Vee Guthrie

Compiled by
Edna
Beilenson

PETER PAUPER PRESS, INC.
WHITE PLAINS · NEW YORK

Greetings!

Mix your batter gaily,
Choose a colored bowl;
Make a cheerful clatter,
Whistle as you roll!

The cookies will be better,
The afternoon less long,
If you do your baking
To a tuneful song!

DROP & MOLD COOKIES

Drop & Mold Cookies

Molasses Cookies

2 ¼ cups sifted flour
1 teaspoon ginger
1 teaspoon cinnamon
¼ teaspoon salt
2 teaspoons baking soda
2 tablespoons hot water
½ cup soft butter
½ cup sugar
½ cup molasses
1 egg
6 tablespoons cold water
½ cup seedless raisins

Sift together first 4 ingredients. Dissolve soda in hot water. Mix butter and next 3 ingredients until creamy; mix in flour mixture alternately with cold water; then mix in soda and all but a few raisins. Drop by tablespoonfuls, 2 inches apart, onto greased cookie sheet. Sprinkle with remaining raisins. Bake in 400° oven 12 minutes. Yields 2 dozen.

If smaller cookies are desired drop dough by teaspoonfuls.

Marmalade Drop Cookies

3 cups sifted flour
½ teaspoon baking soda
½ teaspoon salt
½ cup butter
1 cup sugar
2 eggs, well-beaten
¾ cup orange marmalade

Sift together flour, soda and salt. Cream butter; gradually beat in sugar and eggs; stir in flour, then marmalade. Drop from teaspoon on greased baking sheet, about 2 inches apart, and bake in 350° oven about 12 minutes; remove at once from sheet. Yields 4 dozen cookies.

Sponge Drops

½ cup sifted flour
⅛ teaspoon salt
3 eggs, separated
½ cup sugar
1 tablespoon cold water
½ teaspoon grated lemon rind
¼ teaspoon cream of tartar

Place brown paper on cookie sheet. Sift together first 2 ingredients. Beat egg yolks until thick and lemon-colored;

gradually beat in sugar, then water, rind, flour mixture. Add cream of tartar to egg whites; beat till stiff; fold into yolk mixture. Drop small amounts from teaspoon, 2 inches apart, onto cookie sheet. Bake in 375° oven 12 minutes until golden. Yields 4 to 5 dozen.

Peanut Butter Cookies

   1½ cups sifted flour
   1 teaspoon baking soda
   ½ teaspoon salt
   ½ cup soft butter
   ½ teaspoon vanilla
   ½ cup peanut butter
   ½ cup brown sugar
   ½ cup sugar
   1 unbeaten egg

Sift together flour, soda and salt. Thoroughly mix butter with next 5 ingredients until very light and fluffy. Beat in flour mixture until blended. Form into ½-inch balls. Place 2 inches apart on greased cookie sheets. Bake in 375° oven for 12 minutes until light brown. Yields 75 cookies.

Peanut Butter Chews

   1 can condensed milk
   ½ cup peanut butter
   2 cups fine graham-cracker crumbs
   ½ cup chopped, pitted dates

Mix condensed milk and peanut butter until smooth. Stir in crumbs, and dates. Drop by teaspoonfuls, 1 inch apart, on greased cookie sheet. Bake in 350° oven 15 minutes. Yields 3 dozen.

Peanut Butter Nuggets

1 cup peanut butter
1 teaspoon lemon juice
¼ teaspoon salt
1 can sweetened condensed milk
1 cup chopped raisins

Mix together peanut butter, lemon juice and salt; gradually stir in condensed milk, then raisins. Drop from teaspoon on greased baking sheet and bake in 375° oven about 10 minutes. Yields 3 dozen cookies.

Choco-Cornflake Crisps

In double boiler, melt ½ pound milk chocolate, 1 package semi-sweet chocolate pieces, 2 squares unsweetened chocolate, and 1 tablespoon butter; cool. Chop 1½ cups shredded cocoanut; mix with cooled chocolate mixture; stir in 4 cups corn flakes. Drop onto cookie sheet. Put in refrigerator to set. Yields about 4 dozen.

Cinnamon Nibbles

1 ¼ cups sifted flour
1 teaspoon baking powder
¼ teaspoon salt
½ cup soft butter
1 cup sugar
1 beaten egg
1 teaspoon vanilla
½ cup finely chopped nuts
2 teaspoons cinnamon

Sift together flour, baking powder, salt. Mix, until creamy, butter, sugar, egg, and vanilla. Mix in flour mixture. Chill 1 hour. Shape level tablespoonfuls of dough into balls; roll balls in combined nuts and cinnamon. Arrange on greased cookie sheet, 2 inches apart. Bake in 375° oven 15 minutes. Yields 2 ½ dozen.

Snowdrops

1 cup soft butter
½ cup confectioners' sugar
   (sifted if lumpy)
¼ teaspoon salt
¾ cup finely chopped nuts
2 ¼ cups flour

Mix first 5 ingredients together thoroughly. Work in flour with hands. Chill dough. Roll into small balls about 1 inch in diameter. Bake at 400° on ungreased cookie sheets until set — not brown — about 10-12 minutes. Yields 40 cookies.

Old-Fashioned Soft Cookies

  2 cups sifted flour
  ½ teaspoon baking soda
  ½ teaspoon salt
  ½ cup soft butter
  1 cup sugar
  1 egg yolk
  ½ cup buttermilk or sour milk
  ½ teaspoon vanilla
  1 egg white

Sift together first 3 ingredients. Mix butter, sugar, and egg yolk till fluffy. Mix in flour mixture alternately with buttermilk; then mix in vanilla. Fold in egg white, beaten stiff. Drop by tablespoonfuls, 3 inches apart, onto greased cookie sheet. With spatula, flatten to ½ inch thickness. Bake until golden brown in 375° oven, about 20 minutes. Yields 18 cookies.

The bachelor
  May meet his match
In stirring up
  A cookie batch !

Mincemeat Cookies

    1 cup mincemeat
    3½ cups sifted flour
    1 teaspoon baking soda
    1 teaspoon salt
    ½ teaspoon instant coffee
    1 cup soft butter
    2 cups brown sugar
    2 eggs

Sift together flour and next 3 ingredi-

13

ents. Mix butter with sugar until creamy. Mix in egg, then mincemeat and flour mixture. Drop by teaspoons, 2 inches apart, onto greased cookie sheet. Bake until brown in 400° oven for 12 minutes. Yields 75 cookies.

Oatmeal Cookies

> ¾ cup sifted flour
> ½ teaspoon salt
> ½ teaspoon baking soda
> ½ cup soft butter
> 6 tablespoons brown sugar
> 6 tablespoons granulated sugar
> 1 unbeaten egg
> ¼ teaspoon hot water
> ½ cup chopped walnuts
> 1 package coarsely rolled chilled
>   semi-sweet chocolate pieces
> 1 cup uncooked quick rolled oats
> ½ teaspoon vanilla

Sift flour with salt, soda. Thoroughly mix shortening, sugars, and egg until very light and fluffy. At low speed, beat in remaining ingredients until blended. Drop by teaspoonfuls on ungreased cookie sheet. Bake in 375° oven 12 minutes until done. Yields 4 dozen.

Oatmeal Hermits

1 ½ cups sifted flour
2 teaspoons baking powder
½ teaspoon salt
½ teaspoon cinnamon
2 cups rolled oats
1 cup seeded raisins
½ cup butter
1 cup sugar
2 eggs
½ cup milk

Sift together flour, baking powder, salt and cinnamon; stir in oatmeal and raisins. Cream butter, gradually beat in sugar, then eggs; stir in flour-oatmeal mixture alternately with milk. Drop from teaspoon on greased baking sheet and bake in 375° oven about 15 minutes. Yields 3 dozen cookies.

Gingersnaps

2 cups sifted flour
1 ½ tsp. baking soda
¼ teaspoon salt
1 ½ teaspoons ginger
1 ½ tsp. cinnamon
½ cup butter
½ cup sugar
½ cup molasses
½ cup bran

Sift together dry ingredients. Mix butter, sugar, molasses, until creamy. Add flour mixture, then bran; mix well. Shape, wrap, chill in refrigerator overnight. To bake: Slice dough ⅛ inch thick; place on ungreased cookie sheet. Bake in 375° oven 10 minutes. Yields 5 dozen.

Sour-Cream Jumbles

1 ⅔ cups flour
¼ teaspoon baking soda
1 teaspoon baking powder
½ teaspoon salt
⅓ cup soft butter
⅔ cup sugar
1 egg
½ cup sour cream
½ cup chopped walnuts
¼ teaspoon cinnamon
1 tablespoon granulated sugar

Sift together flour, baking soda, baking powder, and salt. Mix, until creamy, butter, ⅔ cup sugar, and egg. Mix in flour mixture alternately with sour cream; then mix in chopped walnuts. Drop dough by teaspoonfuls, 2 inches apart, onto greased cookie sheet. Combine cinnamon and 1 tablespoon sugar; sprinkle a little on top of each cookie. Bake in 400° oven, 12 minutes, until golden. Yields about 3 dozen.

ROLLING PIN COOKIES

Rolling Pin Cookies

Butter-Rich Cookies

Batter:

2 cups sifted flour
½ teaspoon baking powder
½ teaspoon salt
½ cup butter
1 cup confectioners' sugar
1 egg

Topping:

1 egg
Sugar
Cinnamon
Almonds

Sift flour with baking powder and salt. Then cut butter or margarine into flour mixture with a pastry blender or knife until it looks like corn meal. Then work in sugar and egg. Knead on a lightly floured board until it sticks together. Chill in refrigerator for 20 minutes.

To bake, start oven at 400° or hot. Next roll out the chilled dough on a lightly floured board until it is about ⅛ inch thick. Cut with cookie cutter. Place cookies on a greased cookie sheet, brush with egg (1 whole egg beaten with 2 tablespoons water) and sprinkle with sugar and cinnamon, or with sugar and chopped blanched almonds. Bake for 10 minutes. Cool on wire rack. Yields 60.

Sugar Cookies

  ½ cup soft butter
  ½ cup sugar
  1 egg
  1 tablespoon milk or cream
  ½ teaspoon vanilla
  ½ teaspoon lemon extract
  1 ½ cups flour
  1 teaspoon cream of tartar
  ½ teaspoon soda
  ¼ teaspoon salt

Combine ingredients in above order. Chill dough. Roll out very thin, about 1/16 of an inch. Cut into fancy shapes with cookie cutters — sprinkle with colored sugar and bake at 400° on greased cookie sheets until very lightly browned — about 5-6 minutes. Watch carefully to keep from over-browning. One recipe makes about 80 small cookies.

Ginger Cookies

½ cup shortening
½ cup sugar
½ cup light molasses
½ tablespoon vinegar
1 beaten egg
3 cups enriched flour
¼ teaspoon salt
½ teaspoon soda
½ teaspoon cinnamon
½ teaspoon ginger

Bring shortening, sugar, molasses, and vinegar to boil. Cool and add egg. Add sifted dry ingredients; mix well. Chill. Roll out and cut into rounds. Bake on greased cookie sheet in 375° oven 15 minutes. Yields 30 cookies.

Gingerbread Boys

1¼ cups sifted flour
¾ teaspoon baking soda
½ teaspoon ginger
½ cup molasses
¼ cup soft butter
1 teaspoon grated orange rind

Sift together first 3 ingredients. Bring molasses and shortening to boil in saucepan. Cool slightly; add flour mixture and orange rind; mix well. Chill thoroughly. Roll dough to ⅛-inch thickness. Cut into boy-shapes. Bake on greased cookie sheet, ½ inch apart, 8-10 minutes in 375° oven. Yields 3 dozen.

Molasses Double-Deckers

3 ½ cups sifted flour
1 teaspoon salt
1 teaspoon baking powder
1 teaspoon baking soda
2 teaspoons ginger
½ cup butter
1 cup sugar
2 beaten eggs
½ cup dark molasses
⅓ cup boiling water

Sift together dry ingredients. Cream butter with sugar, then add eggs and molasses. Blend. Add flour mixture alternately with water. When thoroughly mixed, roll out thin on a lightly floured board. Cut half of dough with round cutter. Use doughnut cutter to cut remainder. Bake on cookie sheet in 350° oven 8 to 10 minutes. Cool, put together with a creamy filling or an uncooked frosting. Yields 3 dozen double cookies.

Brown Sugar Cookies

4 eggs
1 pound brown sugar
1 ½ cups flour
1 ½ teaspoons baking powder
1 pinch salt
½ teaspoon vanilla
2 cups pecans
Juice of ½ lemon

Beat eggs and brown sugar together. Cook in double boiler about 20 minutes. When thick, remove. While cooking, measure balance of ingredients. Combine, roll dough out, cut in desired shapes and bake in moderate oven about 25 minutes.

Spekulatius

4 cups flour
1 cup butter
3 eggs
3 ½ cups confectioners' sugar
½ teaspoon cinnamon
Grated rind of 1 lemon
1 teaspoon baking powder

Cream butter and sugar, add eggs one at a time, and continue beating. Mix in the sifted dry ingredients and finally the grated lemon rind. Allow the dough to rest for several hours in a cool place; better still, overnight. Roll out very thin (the old recipe says "no thicker than the back of a knife blade"), cut into fancy shapes and bake in a medium oven, 350°, for 12 to 15 minutes.

Meringue Stars

    1 cup soft butter
    1 egg yolk
    6 tablespoons confectioners' sugar
    3 cups flour
    2 tablespoons sherry
    2 egg whites
    ½ cup granulated sugar
    ⅓-½ cup finely chopped nuts

Combine all ingredients except egg whites, sugar, and nuts. Chill. Roll out to ⅛-¼ inch thickness. Cut out in star shapes with star cookie cutter. Place on slightly greased cookie sheets. Beat egg whites stiff, fold in sugar and heap this meringue in center of each star. Sprinkle nuts on meringue and bake in 325° oven about 25-30 minutes. One recipe makes 60-70 small stars; or 36-40 larger stars. Picturesque Christmas gifts!

Chocolate Butter Cookies

½ cup butter
1 cup sugar
1 egg
2 squares melted and cooled
  unsweetened chocolate
1 teaspoon vanilla
2 cups sifted flour
1 teaspoon double-acting baking
  powder
½ teaspoon salt
Mint- or rum-flavored milk chocolate
  wafers
Bitter-sweet chocolate frosting
Confectioners' sugar frosting
Nuts
Tiny colored candies

Cream butter; add sugar gradually, and continue creaming until light. Add egg; mix well. Add chocolate and vanilla. Stir in sifted dry ingredients. Chill. Roll to ⅛-inch thickness. Cut with floured, fancy cookie cutters. Bake on ungreased cookie sheets in moderate 375° oven, for 8 to 10 minutes. To decorate, put a chocolate wafer on some of cookies, and return to oven for few seconds. While still hot, sandwich some of them. Cool. Decorate others with nuts or candies.

BARS AND SQUARES

Bars & Squares

Apricot Bars

⅔ cup dried apricots
½ cup soft butter
¼ cup sugar
1 cup sifted flour
⅓ cup sifted flour
½ teaspoon baking powder
¼ teaspoon salt
1 cup brown sugar
2 well beaten eggs
½ teaspoon vanilla
½ cup chopped nuts
Confectioners' sugar

Rinse apricots; cover with water; boil 10 minutes. Drain; cool; chop. Heat oven. Grease shallow, square pan. Mix, until crumbly, butter, granulated sugar, and 1 cup flour. Pack into pan. Bake in 350° oven about 25 minutes, or until lightly browned. Sift together ⅓ cup flour, baking powder, salt. Gradually beat brown sugar into eggs. Add flour mixture; mix well. Mix in vanilla, nuts, apricots. Spread over baked layer. Bake 30 minutes, or until done. Cool in pan; cut into bars; roll in confectioners' sugar. Yields 32 bars.

Orange Marmalade Bars

2 ½ cups sifted flour
3 teaspoons baking powder
½ teaspoon salt
¾ cup butter
1 cup sugar
3 well beaten eggs
3 tablespoons orange marmalade
2 tablespoons grated orange rind
1 cup orange juice

Mix and sift flour, baking powder and salt. Cream butter until soft and smooth; gradually add sugar, creaming until fluffy. Beat in eggs, then marmalade and grated orange rind. Add flour alternately with orange juice. Turn into shallow greased baking pan and bake in 350° oven 40 to 50 minutes. When cold, cut in narrow strips; spread with Orange Frosting. Yields 38 strips (1 x 3 inch), or more if cut smaller.

Phyllis' Strudel

2 pounds shortening
2 pounds sugar
1 egg
2 cups sifted flour
1 heaping teaspoon baking powder
Pinch of salt

Cream first 3 ingredients; then add flour, baking powder and salt. Knead until smooth, and form large ball. Chill for a few hours.

Filling:

1 orange rind, grated
1 lemon rind, grated
1 cup walnuts, chopped coarse
½ box seedless raisins
1 cup currant jelly
½ cup cinnamon and sugar, mixed

Grate orange and lemon rind into large bowl. Add all but nuts and cinnamon and sugar mixture.

Roll dough very thin. Brush with oil, sprinkle with cinnamon and sugar mixture liberally. Sprinkle nuts, and spread jelly mixture along center of dough. Roll it up on waxed paper, lightly floured.

28

Place on cookie tin. Spread with egg white. Sprinkle cinnamon, sugar mixture and nuts on top. Press in slightly. Mark for cutting into 1-inch slices. Bake ½ hour in 350° oven. Cut while warm.

Just keep your head,
 Be nimble and quick,
And rolling out cookies
 Is really no trick!

Cinnamon Spice Squares

    1 cup sifted flour
    ½ teaspoon baking powder
    ⅛ teaspoon salt
    2 tablespoons cinnamon
    ½ cup soft butter
    ½ cup sugar
    1 egg
    1 egg, separated
    ½ cup chopped nuts

Sift together first 4 ingredients. Mix, until creamy, butter, sugar, whole egg, and 1 egg yolk. Gradually mix in dry ingredients. Spread in greased square pan. Beat egg white until stiff. Spread over batter; sprinkle with nuts. Bake in 350° oven 15 to 18 minutes until done. Cool in pan; cut into squares. Yields 25 squares.

Scotch Shortbread

    2 cups sifted flour
    ¼ teaspoon baking powder
    ¼ teaspoon salt
    1 cup soft butter
    ½ cup confectioners' sugar

Sift together first 3 ingredients. Mix

butter and sugar until creamy. Add flour mixture; blend. Chill. Heat oven. On lightly-floured, cloth-covered board, roll dough to ¼-inch thickness. Cut into squares. Place on ungreased cookie sheet, 1 inch apart. Bake in 350° oven 20 to 25 minutes or until done. Before baking, if desired, sprinkle cinnamon-and-sugar mixture on cookies.

Oatmeal Molasses Cookies

2 cups sifted flour
1 teaspoon baking soda
1 teaspoon salt
½ teaspoon cinnamon
¼ teaspoon cloves
2½ cups quick-cooking oats
¾ cup butter
½ cup sugar
½ cup molasses
1 beaten egg
¼ cup milk
1 cup seedless raisins

Sift together flour, baking soda, salt and spices and stir in oats. Cream shortening; gradually stir in sugar and molasses, beating thoroughly. Add egg and mix

well. Add milk, then flour, beating well.
Fold in raisins and bake in lightly buttered rectangular pan in 375° oven 12
to 15 minutes, or until done. Cut into
squares. Yields 5 dozen.

Chocolate Peanut Butter Squares

1 cup sifted flour
1 teaspoon baking powder
¼ teaspoon baking soda
¼ teaspoon salt
2 tablespoons butter
1 cup sugar
1 egg
½ cup peanut butter
1 square melted chocolate
¼ cup milk

Sift together flour, baking powder, soda
and salt. Beat together butter, sugar and
egg; then stir in peanut butter and
chocolate; gradually stir in flour alternately with milk. Bake in greased pan
in 375° oven about 15 minutes. Cut in
squares. Yields 2 dozen.

Please note: For best results in cutting brownies, hermits, and other soft cookie squares, allow to cool slightly in pan before cutting. Use a sharp knife, and cut firmly while still warm.

Brownies are a great favorite for lunch boxes, or packages-from-home.

Play a bar ♪ ♩ ♪ ♩
And dance a square:
Bake them here
And eat them there!

Brownies

⅔ cup sifted flour
½ teaspoon baking powder
¾ teaspoon salt
1 cup granulated sugar
½ cup soft butter
2 eggs
1 teaspoon vanilla
2 squares melted unsweetened
  chocolate
1 cup chopped walnuts

Sift together first 3 ingredients. Gradually add sugar to shortening, mixing until light. Add eggs, vanilla; mix smooth. Blend in chocolate, then flour mixture and nuts. Turn into greased pan. Bake in 350° oven 30 minutes. Cool in pan; cut into squares. Yields 16 squares.

Brown Sugar Brownies

2 eggs
1 ¼ cups brown sugar
1 teaspoon vanilla
2 squares melted bitter chocolate
½ cup sifted flour
1 cup chopped walnuts

Beat eggs until thick. Gradually beat in

sugar, vanilla, chocolate. Mix in flour, then half of nuts. Turn into greased shallow pan; top with rest of nuts. Bake in 350° oven 25 to 30 minutes until done. Cool in pan; cut. Yields 16 squares.

Jiffy Brownies

  2 cups graham-cracker crumbs
  ½ cup chopped walnuts
  1 teaspoon vanilla
  1 can condensed milk
  ¼ teaspoon salt
  1 package semi-sweet chocolate pieces

Mix cracker crumbs well with rest of ingredients. Turn into greased shallow pan; bake in 350° oven 25 to 30 minutes until done. Cut while warm.

Butterscotch Brownies

  1½ cups sifted flour
  2 teaspoons baking powder
  ½ cup butter
  2 cups brown sugar
  2 eggs
  1 teaspoon vanilla
  1 cup chopped nuts

Grease and flour shallow, rectangular

pan. Sift flour with baking powder. Melt butter in heavy pan over low heat; add sugar; bring to boil, stirring. Cool till lukewarm. Drop in eggs, one at a time, mixing well. Mix in vanilla, flour mixture, nuts. Turn into pan. Bake in 350° oven 30 to 35 minutes. Cool in pan; cut. Yields 24.

"No-Cook" Squares

¼ cup melted butter or margarine
½ cup corn syrup
1 cup sifted confectioners' sugar
Dash of salt
⅔ cup cocoa
1 6-oz. box sugar crisps (cereal)
1 cup coarsely chopped nuts
⅔ cup coarsely cut cocoanut

Combine butter, syrup, sugar, salt, and cocoa in a large bowl. Mix well. Then add the other ingredients, and with a large fork, stir until cereal is well coated. Pack mixture firmly into a greased 12 x 8 x 2-inch pan. Chill in refrigerator until firm. Cut into squares. To keep cookies crisp, store in refrigerator. Makes 3 to 4 dozen.

Date and Nut Chews

¾ cup sifted flour
¾ teaspoon baking powder
1 cup sugar
¼ teaspoon salt
1 cup finely cut dates
1 cup chopped walnuts
2 beaten eggs

Mix together first 4 ingredients. Add dates, nuts, eggs. Mix thoroughly. Spread in shallow pan. Bake at 350° about 45 minutes. Cut into small squares. Yields 4 dozen.

37

Southern Pecan Sticks

½ cup soft butter
1½ cups sifted flour
¼ teaspoon salt
1 tablespoon granulated sugar
1 egg
2 tablespoons water
2 eggs
1 cup brown sugar
2 tablespoons flour
½ teaspoon baking powder
½ teaspoon salt
½ teaspoon vanilla
1 cup chopped pecans

Mix first 4 ingredients to the consistency of fine corn meal. Mix in 1 egg and water. Press into shallow, rectangular baking dish. Bake 15 minutes in 350° oven. Beat 2 eggs; add rest of ingredients; mix well. Spread over baked layer; bake 40 minutes. Cool in dish; cut into sticks. Yields 32 sticks.

Date Sticks

Heat oven to 325° and grease 12″ x 8″ x 2″ baking dish. Sift together into bowl:

1 ⅓ cups granulated sugar
1 ½ cups sifted enriched flour
1 teaspoon baking powder
1 teaspoon salt

Then mix in:

2 tablespoons milk
2 beaten eggs

Finally, add:

1 cup chopped walnuts
1 package cut-up pitted dates
1 teaspoon vanilla

Bake at 325° 30 minutes, or until done.
Cut into sticks while still warm.

Hazelnut Slices

1 ⅓ cups sifted flour	½ cup butter
⅓ cup sugar	1 egg white
⅛ teaspoon ginger	½ cup hazelnuts

Sift flour, sugar and ginger together;
cut in butter. Add egg white and work
to a smooth dough. Add chopped nuts,
shape into roll and wrap in waxed paper.
Chill in refrigerator 2 hours. Slice ¼
inch thick. Bake in 350° oven 12 to 15
minutes, or until slightly browned.
Yields 40 cookies.

Cookie Frosting

Bittersweet Chocolate Frosting: Melt 1 ½ squares unsweetened chocolate; cool. Boil 3 tablespoons sugar and 2 tablespoons water until sugar is dissolved. Cool. Stir into chocolate. Let stand until thickened.

This cookie frosting is excellent on gift cookies.

SPECIAL GIFT
COOKIES

Special Gift Cookies

Fudge Cookies, Supreme

1½ cups sifted flour
¼ cup granulated sugar
½ teaspoon baking powder
½ teaspoon salt
½ cup semi-sweet chocolate pieces
½ cup chopped pecans
¼ cup soft butter
1 beaten egg
Granulated sugar

Sift together flour, sugar, baking powder and salt. In double boiler, combine chocolate, pecans, butter. Heat over hot water until chocolate is melted; then stir until smooth. Remove from heat; cool slightly. Add egg; mix thoroughly. Add flour mixture; mix well. Place dough on waxed paper; shape, wrap, and chill in refrigerator overnight. To bake: Slice dough ⅛ inch thick; place on ungreased cookie sheet. Sprinkle with sugar. Bake at 375° 10 minutes. Cool before removing from cookie sheet. Yields 2½ dozen.

English Brandy Snaps

¾ cup butter
¾ cup sugar
½ cup molasses
1 ½ cups sifted flour
2 teaspoons ginger

Heat butter, sugar and molasses until blended. Add ginger. Remove from heat, add flour, beating until smooth. Drop from tip of spoon on greased baking sheet, about 2 inches apart. Bake in 300° oven about 12 minutes. Quickly remove from pan and roll at once, top side out, over handle of a wooden spoon. Yields 4 dozen wafers.

Petticoat Tails

Mix together 1 cup soft shortening, 1 cup sifted confectioners' sugar, and 1 teaspoon vanilla or almond extract. Add 1 ½ cups sifted flour, ¼ teaspoon salt. Knead, shape, wrap, chill in refrigerator overnight. Cut dough into thin slices; place on ungreased cookie sheet. Bake in 400° oven 8-10 minutes. Yields 5 dozen.

Pinwheel Cookies

4½ cups sifted flour
1 teaspoon salt
1 teaspoon baking soda
1 teaspoon cinnamon
1 cup butter
2 cups brown sugar
½ cup granulated sugar
3 eggs

Sift flour, salt, baking soda, cinnamon together. Work butter until soft, then work in both sugars gradually until smooth. Add unbeaten eggs and beat hard. Mix dry ingredients into creamed mixture thoroughly. Chill several hours in refrigerator while you make the *Filling:* Cook 1½ cups ground raisins, 1 cup sugar, 1 cup water over a low heat until mixture is thick. Stir constantly. Remove from heat and stir in ½ cup chopped nuts. Cool; then chill.

Divide dough in half and roll ¼-inch thick on lightly floured board. Spread with an even layer of filling (both dough and filling must be very cold to roll neatly). Roll dough as in making jelly roll and wrap in waxed paper. Store overnight in refrigerator. Cut in ⅛-inch slices, place 1 inch apart on greased cookie sheets and bake in a 375° oven for 10 to 15 minutes. Yields 6 dozen.

Postman ! Postman !
What have you got ?
A package of cookies -
Not a crumb
On the lot !

Brown Lace Cookies

2 cups brown sugar
¼ cup butter
2 eggs, well beaten
½ pound pecans, cut coarse
½ cup flour
1 teaspoon vanilla
1 teaspoon baking powder

Cream butter and sugar, add eggs, beat well, add vanilla. Add the baking powder to flour and mix with nuts, and combine the two mixtures. Place in the refrigerator until firm, 1 hour or more.

Drop by ½ teaspoonfuls 3 inches apart on buttered and floured tin. Bake at 400° until golden brown. Remove from the pan when slightly cooled.

Icebox Nut Wafers

1¼ cups flour	1 cup brown sugar
¼ teaspoon salt	1 egg
½ tsp. baking soda	½ teaspoon vanilla
½ cup butter	½ cup nuts

Sift flour, salt, baking soda together. Work butter until soft. Work in sugar gradually until smooth. Beat in the egg. Now stir in dry ingredients, vanilla and chopped nuts. Divide dough in half. Shape into long rolls on a lightly-floured board. Wrap in waxed paper and refrigerate overnight.

Cut in very thin slices. Place on greased cookie sheets and bake in a 375° oven for 7 to 10 minutes. Yields 5 dozen cookies.

Tea Cookies

½ cup soft butter
¼ cup sugar
1 egg yolk
1 teaspoon vanilla
1 tablespoon grated orange rind
1 teaspoon lemon juice
1 ¼ cups sifted flour
⅛ teaspoon salt
1 egg white
¾ cup chopped nuts
Candied cherries

Mix, until creamy, butter, sugar, egg yolk, vanilla, orange rind, and lemon juice. Add flour and salt; mix. Chill until easy to handle; form into 1-inch balls.

Heat oven. Dip balls in unbeaten egg white; roll in nuts. Place on greased cookie sheet, 2 inches apart. Press cherry half into top of each. Bake in 350° oven 20 to 25 minutes. Yields 3½ dozen.

Icebox Orange Cookies

2½ cups sifted flour
3 teaspoons baking powder
¼ teaspoon salt
½ cup butter
1 cup sugar
1 egg
Grated rind 1 orange
¼ cup orange juice

Sift flour, baking powder, salt, together. Work butter until soft and work in the sugar gradually until smooth. Beat in well-beaten egg and orange rind, then mix in the sifted dry ingredients alternately with orange juice.

Divide dough in half and shape into rolls on lightly floured board. Wrap in waxed paper. Chill in refrigerator overnight. Slice ⅛ inch thick and place on greased cookie sheets. Bake in a 375° oven for 10 to 12 minutes. Yields 6 dozen.

COOKIES FROM FOREIGN LANDS

Foreign Cookies

Kris Kringles

½ cup butter
¼ cup sugar
1 beaten egg yolk
1 tablespoon grated orange peel
1 teaspoon grated lemon peel
1 teaspoon lemon juice
1 cup flour
⅛ teaspoon salt
1 slightly beaten egg white
½ cup chopped walnuts
10 candied cherries

Cream shortening and sugar; add egg yolk, orange and lemon peel, and lemon juice. Beat thoroughly. Stir in flour and salt. Chill until firm. Form small balls about ½ inch in diameter. Dip in egg white and roll lightly in nuts. Place on greased cookie sheet; press ½ candied cherry in center of each. Bake in moderate oven (325°) about 20 minutes. Yields 20.

Viennese Crescents

1 cup soft butter
⅓ cup granulated sugar
⅔ cup chopped almonds
¼ teaspoon salt
1 ⅔ cups flour

Mix first 4 ingredients together thoroughly — then work in flour with hands. Chill dough. Pull off small pieces of chilled dough and work with hands until pliable but not sticky. Roll between palms into pencil-thick strips and shape into small crescents on ungreased cookie sheets. Bake at 375° until set — not brown (about 15 minutes.) Remove from cookie sheets when cooled and roll in confectioners' sugar. Yields 75 cookies.

Viennese Linzer Cookies

Mix together, until creamy, 1 cup soft butter, 1 cup granulated sugar, and 2 egg yolks. Add 1 teaspoon grated lemon rind, 2 cups sifted flour, 1 cup ground almonds; ¾ teaspoon cinnamon, ½ teaspoon powdered cloves; mix well. Chill 1 hour. Heat oven. Roll between 2 sheets

of waxed paper to ⅛-inch thickness.
Cut into 2-inch rounds; spread with
jam; top with crisscross strips of dough.
Place on ungreased cookie sheet. Bake
in 400° oven 12 to 15 minutes. Yields
5 dozen cookies.

German Anise Drops

   2 eggs
   1 cup sugar
   1 teaspoon anise seeds
   1 ¼ cups flour

Beat eggs and sugar together for 20 minutes (by hand or in electric mixer at low
speed.) Add anise seeds and stir in the
flour gradually. Drop by half teaspoonfuls on greased cookie sheets. Let these
stand overnight or at least 8 hours before baking. Bake in 325° oven until
cookies are pale yellow color on the bot-
tom (about 12 minutes.) If cookies get
too hard in the storing process put a
couple of pieces of white bread in the tin
with the cookies. This will soften them
somewhat. One recipe makes 45 or more
1 ½-inch cookies.

Lebkuchen

1 pound sugar
1 pound ground almonds
5 medium eggs
3 ounces chopped lemon peel
1 grated lemon rind
½ ground nutmeg
1 teaspoon cinnamon
Dash ground cloves

Beat sugar, whole eggs and grated lemon rind for ½ hour, add spices, finally the

Freeze them in ice,
Bake them in heat,
And store them for
A special treat!

almonds. Drop the dough by spoonfuls onto a buttered tin; bake cookies to a golden brown. Top with an icing of confectioners' sugar stirred smooth with the juice of a lemon. Sprinkle with colored sugar beads.

Hungarian Ragalach

    1 cup soft sweet butter
    ½ pound soft cream cheese
    ¼ teaspoon salt
    2 cups sifted flour
    1 cup chopped walnuts
    ½ cup granulated sugar
    1 tablespoon cinnamon

Mix butter, cheese, and salt until creamy. Mix in flour. Shape into 14 balls. Chill overnight. Heat oven. On lightly floured, cloth-covered board, roll each ball to 6-inch circle. Cut each into quarters. Mix nuts, sugar, cinnamon. Drop rounded teaspoonful on each quarter. Pinch together edges of dough; then form into crescents. Place on ungreased cookie sheet. Bake till light brown in a 350° oven for about 12 minutes. Yields about 50 cookies.

Swedish Sprits

1½ cups butter
1 cup sugar
1 well beaten egg
2 teaspoons vanilla
4 cups flour
1 teaspoon baking powder

Thoroughly cream butter and sugar; add egg and vanilla. Beat well. Add sifted dry ingredients, mix to smooth dough. Force through cookie press, forming various shapes. Or roll, cut out and emboss. Bake in hot oven (400°) until light brown — about 8 to 10 minutes.

Sandbakelser
(Sand Tarts)

⅓ cup blanched almonds
⅞ cup soft butter
¾ cup sugar
1 unbeaten small egg white
2 cups enriched flour

Put almonds through fine knife of food grinder twice. Thoroughly mix in butter, sugar, and unbeaten egg white. Then stir in flour. Chill dough. Press dough into Sandbakelser molds (or tiny, fluted tart forms) to coat inside. Place on ungreased baking sheet. Bake in a moderate oven (350°) until very delicately browned, about 12 to 15 minutes. Tap molds on table to loosen cookies and turn them out of the molds. Yields about 36 cookies.

Danish Vanilla Cookies

2½ cups sifted flour
½ teaspoon baking powder
1 cup sugar
1 cup butter
2 slightly beaten egg yolks
1½ teaspoons vanilla

Sift together flour, baking powder and sugar; cut in butter until well mixed. Stir in egg yolks and vanilla and work dough until smooth; chill. Roll thin on lightly floured board and cut as desired, or force through a cookie press on ungreased baking sheet. Bake in 375°-400° oven 10 to 12 minutes. For more festive cookies, brush shapes with slightly beaten egg whites and sprinkle with chopped nuts or plain or colored sugar. Yields 4 to 5 dozen cookies.

Swedish Nut Dreams

6 eggs, separated
1 ¼ cups granulated sugar
3 ½ cups finely ground walnuts
3 teaspoons almond extract

Beat yolks until thick and tripled in volume. Add sugar, beating until thick. Fold in nuts and extract. Beat whites until stiff; fold into yolk mixture. Bake in pan lined with greased paper at 325° for 1 hour. Cool 10 minutes and turn out; remove paper; cool. Cut as needed. Yields 30.

Scandinavian Stars

- ½ cup maple syrup
- ½ cup butter
- ⅓ cup brown sugar
- 1 teaspoon ginger
- 1 teaspoon cinnamon
- 1 teaspoon powdered cloves
- 1 teaspoon grated lemon rind
- 1 tablespoon dark rum
- 1 teaspoon baking soda
- 2½ cups sifted flour

Boil together first 3 ingredients until butter and sugar are melted. Mix in ginger and next 5 ingredients. Cool to lukewarm. Gradually mix in flour. Chill for 1 hour. Heat oven. On lightly floured, cloth-covered board, roll dough paper-thin. Cut with stars. Bake on greased cookie sheet in 350° oven 5 to 8 minutes. Yields 6 dozen.

Almond Croissants

- ½ cup butter
- ½ cup sugar
- ⅛ teaspoon salt
- 2 egg yolks
- ¼ cup finely chopped almonds

1 cup sifted flour
1 egg white
1 teaspoon water
Chopped almonds

Cream together butter, sugar, and salt; beat in egg yolks, then finely chopped almonds. Gradually stir in flour until dough is stiff enough to handle; chill thoroughly. Roll ⅛-inch thick on lightly floured board; cut with small crescent-shaped cutter and place on greased baking sheet. Brush with egg white and water beaten together until frothy; sprinkle with chopped almonds and bake in 375° oven 12 minutes. Yields 1½ dozen cookies.

French Meringues

1 cup granulated sugar
½ cup water
2 egg whites
⅛ teaspoon almond extract
¼ teaspoon vanilla
½ cup ground, blanched almonds

Heat oven. Boil sugar with water to 265° (hard, almost brittle ball). Beat whites till stiff; then pour in sugar syrup in fine stream, beating constantly. When mixture holds its shape, fold in extracts and almonds. Drop by teaspoonfuls onto well-greased cookie sheet, and bake in 250° oven about 15 minutes. Yields about 50 meringues.

English Teacakes

    1¾ cups sifted flour
    1½ teaspoons baking powder
    ¼ teaspoon salt
    ¼ cup soft shortening
    ¼ cup soft butter
    ¾ cup granulated sugar
    1 egg
    3 tablespoons milk
    ½ cup chopped citron
    ½ cup currants or raisins
    1 slightly beaten egg white
    Granulated sugar

Sift together flour, baking powder and salt. Mix, until creamy, shortening, butter, sugar, and egg. Add milk, citron, currants, and flour mixture; mix well. Chill. Heat oven. Roll dough into balls the size of walnuts. Dip tops into egg white, then sugar. Place with sugared sides up, 2 inches apart, on greased cookie sheet. Bake till golden in a 400°

oven, about 15 minutes. Yields about 35 cookies.

Chinese Almond Cookies

2½ cups flour
¾ cup granulated sugar
¼ teaspoon salt
1 teaspoon baking powder
¾ cup soft butter
1 egg
2 tablespoons water
1 teaspoon almond extract
⅓ cup blanched almonds
1 egg yolk
1 tablespoon water

Sift together first 4 ingredients. Mix shortening and egg until creamy. Add 2 tablespoons water and extract; mix. Gradually add flour mixture, stirring with fork till mixture draws away from sides of bowl. Knead to blend; chill 1 hour. Heat oven. Form dough into 1-inch balls; using palm of hand, flatten each to ¼-inch thickness. Place on greased cookie sheet, ½ inch apart. Press almond in each; brush with yolk beaten with 1 tablespoon water. Bake in 350° oven, 25 minutes. Yields 3 dozen.